Coupon Envy
The Secrets to Extreme Couponing

Coupon Envy History

In 2010 I was placed in a position that became apparent I needed to learn to budget and save money more wisely; quickly. At the time I was sheltering a four member family along with my two children. Having them down on their luck I tried to help as much as possible but it was making an undue hardship on my personal finances. After searching the internet for "grocery store savings." I was reminded of coupon cutting. As a teenager my after school job was at a local Scott's (Kroger) grocery store. As I sat there staring at the computer monitor a vivid memory crossed my mind. One particular customer would come in and

send no more than 10% retail. I always felt like I had made a mistake in the transaction and would recheck the math. Then customers were allowed to use competitor's ads and store coupons along with manufacturer's coupons. Limit two coupons and one cut out per item. (As I still remember the policy from then). I the math nerd and her a numbers whiz mastered the cash register every time she visited the store. By using a complex combination of manufacturer coupon + store coupon + competitor ad = HUGE SAVINGS, every time.

Within months of deciding to attempt the task, TLC released a show called Extreme Couponing. At that moment I knew I was on the right track to saving the money I needed. All the while learning to follow a strict budget and buying plan. Following tips from that original airing I frantically taught myself to do exactly what I saw on TV and remembered from my childhood. After several disappointing attempts I finally took my curiosity to the internet. Knowing what I know now; I have no idea how my favorite customer did this without the internet. I wouldn't have had the patience.

Shortly after graduating high school I began working for Wells Fargo Bank. I was trained on every possible personal bank account there was available at the time. This is where I also learned the joy of sales, marketing, and advertising. I since have spent several years between sales and customer services with leading companies in competitive industries. I not only have the personal expertise on the benefits of coupon clipping but I also have the employment experience to make sure each of you remain satisfied.

I am a mother of two young men, ages 20 and 13. Both out grew me by the time they were 12. With that being said, that is why I still coupon! So, let's get to business.

Dedications

Unlike most authors I saved this page for last. It was the hardest part of the book to write. It tugged at my emotions, my heart, and my soul. I was lost for the right words to fill this page with. Once, I was with the last edit I knew what I wanted to say.

Dear Tiffany Ellis,

Being the older sister, I was tasked with watching after you, which I did with pride. The pretty, smart and at times quiet, younger version of our mother. I used to watch your face panic when you got too high on the swings at the park. Only to giggle with you as the swing headed back toward the ground. That laugh was contagious. Your giggle, soul relaxing. Your unapproved walks to the candy store by yourself, scared me to the core. I always wanted to protect you. I always wanted to be there when you did your best. I always wanted to jump in the way of any harm that came your way. I can't say we didn't have our sibling fights, of course we did. All siblings do. What I can say is, through all of them our relationship grew stronger. At times as, a kid I wished I had a big sister. Someone to treat me and protect me like I did for you. I used to wish you were older, so we could share some of the same experiences together. That wasn't the case, you four years younger never shared a school with me. For years no one knew, "that's Tonya's little sister." I bragged about you all the time. I knew you would grow to have the most loving soul of us all. I was right.

Tiffany, you are ever supporting of all I do. Years ago, you told me to start this journey. To be honest I was afraid to. I didn't believe I could do it. Yes, everyone gives me the credit because that's my pen name printed on the cover. Yet, you and I know the truth. Without you none of this would have ever happened. Without you I wouldn't have believed in myself. Without you it'd still just be an idea. I used to want a big sister to guide me; I instead have a little sister who encourages me without limit. I have a little sister who believes in me. I have a little sister who is undoubtedly proud of me. I never have to question that with you. I never have to question your sincerity, loyalty or dependability. I was blessed to have you.

So, before you cry reading this I want to make clear, thank you for believing in me when I didn't believe in myself. I love you baby sis and this book is completely because of you. I dedicate this writing to the bond of sisterhood, which you've so graciously blessed me with.

Your Big Little Sis

To my unpaid manager, confidant, and mentor Joe B. Hall: your guidance is truly appreciated. I love you for being there at any time to answer my call. Without measure, thank you.

To my loving mother Diane R Young: MOMMA SAID! (Wink) There are no words that will ever grace this page to show my true appreciation for all you've done. I only hope to one day be more like you. I love you and am so proud to call you mom. Thank you for all your love and support, being your child is the best thing a girl could ask for.

To my children Tayvon and Tyrese: Mom does it all for you. You're both my motivation and what keeps me going daily. From the beginning you both have helped me through this process. Tayvon, you have shown me your determination to support my dreams and I am proud of the man you are becoming. Tyrese, thank you for always helping and checking in on me while I worked. I truly have the best kids in the world. I wouldn't ask for anything more if all I had where you two.

Contents

Intro

Being you are reading this you have already taken the necessary steps to learn a proven and successful way to save your family money. We have all experienced that moment of temptation when making purchases to break the budget. We have all searched for ways to save money, which is what directed you to this course. Learning the basics of extreme couponing you will soon be able to save money on every day purchases. Ironically this leads to being a more consistence consumer on all purchases both large and small. Since I began couponing I have saved money on my utilities, car purchases and even travel. I accomplish these savings by being more aware of retail and suggested pricing on most things sold in this country. I have also learned the skill of price competition. This is when Walmart and Kroger battle it out over that last little penny to get you in store. Kroger has an item for sale at $19.97 whereas, Walmart everyday low price of $19.98. Price competition is only one way for products and services to compete. Being this world deals in numbers and letters, the lower price usually wins the competition. Until couponing!

Couponing is based not only on low advertised price but several other aspects that will ultimately alter the final price, putting the savings in your pocket. When shopping and looking for deals you must remember the suggested or retail prices. This will ensure you are using the actual lowest price per serving. Going forward you will rarely shop by price without first looking at serving sizes. Everything we purchase has weight, and that weight is what manufacturers use to validate and price inventory. You can save money on many of your purchases by simply being a more aware and prepared consumer.

Couponing has become a trend that has nothing to do with status quo or economic shortcomings. It has grew to be more of a lifestyle change than people originally predicted. When discussing coupons one must visually think of "funny money." Think of a coupon as a form of payment, hence having a face value. Viewing coupons as holding monetary value you soon execute using them for full benefit. Although coupons are also known as: cut-out, printable, and/or tear tab. We will refer to them as coupons throughout this course.

Next, you find an example of a coupon and the explanation of its details. As shown they are very detailed legal documents and should NOT be altered, copied, or destroyed. Coupons are used by the store to receive payment for the discount carried out to the customer at purchase as requested (the coupon is a manufacturer's request to discount an item/product/service). Do stores send physical box loads of coupons for payment? Short answer, no. However, this is why most coupons have some sort of identifying markings and/or barcodes. Let it be watermarks or offset margins; they are not easily duplicated. The first example is a fraudulent coupon. Although not easily duplicated, people have and obviously will attempt to defraud two companies for the benefit of a cheap or free product. That you should hold no respect for nor attempt. The second example you see a legitimate coupon authorized to be printed from the internet. These coupons work the same as a cut out or clipped coupon. Can you see the difference?

Photo credit: southernsavers.com and print.coupons.com

With a basic understanding of what a coupon should look like, the next question on your mind should be: who accepts coupons? Legally anyone selling a product that has a corresponding coupon can be reimbursed for the discount given of said item through submission of the coupon. This submission can be electronic or physical request. From small ma and pop stores to major supply chains and in between, most accept coupons in one form or another. Coupons were based on the concept of increased revenue, product recognition and lastly consumer retention. The appearance of a coupon gives the sense that it is meant for the customer to benefit when in actuality it is just the opposite. Manufacturers release coupons with the hopes of winning price competition not customer savings. Whereas, a store offers a sale with the same goals in plan. When manufactures and stores meet together this is the perfect timing for couponing. This is when the consumer can and will win; if planned correctly. Just as a business has a business plan for strategy and success, the consumer should have a buyer and protection plan at all times. Remember price competition benefits the company not the consumer. It is simply a visual effect of offering a sale price and/or coupon that gives the false sense of savings. Have you ever wondered why coupon savings are frequently based off packaging, serving, size, and/or quantity? This is an attempt by store and/or manufacturer to control your purchase resulting in them getting the better revenue over its competitors on similar items, products, and services.

As mentioned there are several different types of coupons; the key is who reimburses the coupon. For the most part and for the sake of this course. Coupons are distributed by one or both of these entities: the store of purchase and the manufacturer of product. Knowing and identifying the store coupons are easily done. Simply use the digital, electronic, and/or printable rewards programs. Even gas stations have these programs now; USE THEM! Identifying a manufacturer can be a

little difficult without a little research or coupon in hand. An example of this is; the manufacturer of Tide and Gain products is Procter and Gamble. Although you've unknowingly seen their logos and advertisements, those references are not how most consumers identify their favorite products. Which again is the genius of the manufacturing companies. Not wanting to appear as a monopolized company, manufacturers sell products under different brands, labels and names. Rest assured, as smart as the manufactures may seem at this point, they are an entity of ethics and regulations. You are a walking, thinking, and performing human being. You can always win against made up numbers thought out over an hour worth of sales and marketing meetings. Be confident in; there are more of us to out think them than there is in the sales meetings on Monday.

An in-store coupon is a lot easier to identify and use in most cases. Very rarely will a store not accept their own coupon (form of payment). It's like taking money from your right pocket and putting it in your left for more security. Didn't make sense? Neither, does a store not accepting their own method of payment presented in coupon form. In-store coupons cannot typically be combined with other in-store coupons for a single item. However, they can be combined with manufacturers' coupons. This combination is what leads to extreme couponing and your basic everyday savings goal. When applying this combination method into your shopping you will easily save up to 50% at the grocery store. If you go even further and apply this method in large quantities then you've become an extreme couponer.

As previously mentioned stores offer a lot of their advertised discounts and coupons through some means of electronic form. Shopper reward programs also known as loyalty programs are designed to offer the consumer rewards, points, perks, coupons, and much more for shopping with at their locations. Some are as easy as entering your phone number or swiping a card at the register. Whereas, others have evolved into smart phone apps requiring login and personal information sharing. Thinking back again to my favorite customer; she never had to share her information to get coupons so why should I? I rarely do. You can easily make a new email account strictly for coupons and shopper reward programs. Just be sure to remember the login information. When using shopper reward programs and point this can become very complicated. There are several restrictions when using earned points as well as when earning points. This brings us to the absolute necessity of knowing and following the store's coupon policy. Make it a point to regularly check the store's policy before planning a shopping trip. Doing this simple task prior to planning a trip will save you time and lower the risk of a failed purchase. There is nothing more embossing than to think you will be spending less than $10 but for some reason your total is still showing $100. It has happened to the best of us and more times than none it is because of the coupon policy on reward programs.

Tips: Plan before you shop. Identify manufacturer vs. in-store coupons. Register for store and loyalty programs. Become familiar with store coupon policies and check them regularly.

Coupon Clipping and Printing
What coupons do I need?
Where do I find coupons?
Clipped vs. Printed
Why didn't they take my coupon?
When planning a shopping trip be sure you have the correct accompanying coupons per item. Remember coupons are based per item, weight and/or total. This will come in handy when doing an extreme purchase. Taking the time to make sure you have the correct coupons is key to knowing the outcome of your purchase before the final total button is pressed on the register. Being prepared is the only way I know how to shop. I often tell my attendees: when you purchase a car you look for the best deals comparing prices, options, and benefits. Why not have that same actions when purchasing gum at the checkout. We put so much thought into big purchases failing to realize at times, it is the smaller everyday purchases that truly determine our budgets. Without a budget on groceries, entertainment, and disposables you wouldn't be able to afford the nice car, big house or relaxing vacations. Getting ahold of those smaller purchases will in turn make more liquid equity available for large purchases. Having that thought process will affect your buying habits and in turn you will start seeing savings with minimum effort.
Knowing coupons are accepted on a per item basis, making sure every item has a coupon will ensures savings usually around 20%-50%. Manufacturers and stores alike communicate with one another well ahead of time about price changes and upcoming sales. Therefore, stores will purposely plan a sale of their own. This goes full circle to price competition. The store is aware the manufacturer is going to offer some form of discount. With millions of stores and distributors they must remain competitive during these times as to record profit at the store level. The ultimate goal is not minimum effort, results, or saving; the goal is extreme. When extreme couponing the shopper must have at least a manufacturer's coupon, in-store coupon or special, and shopper reward bonus. Any combination of these items for each product will result in extreme savings per item progressing to extreme purchasing power. I.e. Bulk buying. Registering between 80%-100% is the total goal for this level of couponing. Extreme couponing requires time, dedication, basic math skills, patience and most importantly self-control. Couponing to the extreme is highly addictive because of the urge to get items at a near free cost every time. It is certainty with extreme levels of effort comes extreme couponing and, extreme savings.

Locating coupons is a fairly easy task however getting them in your hand can be time consuming. I have tried every avenue of getting coupons and I still have prime results (see resources page). I hear time and time again that it is hard to coupon since there is not many places that multiply (double) coupons. This is not true at all. Recalling my favorite customer again, I remember a small yet crucial detail. Her trick was dollar coupons combined with in-store coupons and competitor cut-outs (these were used for price matching). Do not be misled that because an item has an available coupon that means it's also on sale. This is not always true and in most cases isn't on sale. Here's an example of why doubling and tripling coupons is not a requirement for extreme couponing. Just to sooth any false perceptions of inability. With companies discounting the doubling and tripling of coupons the number of loyalty and cash back programs have increased. Knowing how to utilize these programs is how you self-supply the doubling and tripling power of coupons you choose.

Many times the misconception is if separate purchases are made than the price will eventually cause an overage. This wasn't always true, with multiplying. Most times the best benefits came when an item was on sale for less than $2.00. Remembering back in 2010 coupon multiplying restrictions were limited to up to 50¢ off for tripling and $1.00 for doubling with only the first two like coupons multiplying. Extreme levels of couponing came when the coupon final discount was more than the item cost. This allowed for non-coupon holding items (i.e. Deli, butcher, floral) to be purchased and in some cases cash back in hand at the register. Those were the good old days. The savings can still be accomplished with some extra work. Very rarely now will a couponer receive cash back at the register. Now managers are directed to have consumer purchase something of that credit balance. When that happens a savings of 100% on a large purchase is just as rewarding as receiving cash back on a smaller purchase.

Overcoming misconceptions like those is common when one correctly knows their coupon buying limits. Each coupon will have restrictions, as well as the store that accepts it. All coupons must be read prior to usage, likewise the store coupon policy must be verified regularly. The reasons you want to verify stores' coupon policy is to learn transaction limits, combining rules, and coupon quantity restrictions. A store can limit the amount of transactions you perform daily, this is a transaction limit. Example, Dollar General regularly limits the amount of transactions that can be made to 2-4 per day. The store's combining rules are key to extreme couponing. As stated, you want to combine specials, sales, rewards, and coupons for each item. Meijer has a rule stating you can't use a digital coupon and a physical coupon on the same item, regardless if they are the different. Lastly, manufacturers and stores alike can limit the amount of like coupons used in a single transaction. Many times you will receive a manufacturer coupon stating limit 4 like coupons in single transaction. This simply means you can only use four of those same coupons per transaction. It however does not limit the amount of transactions you can make. Which is why you verify the store policy on transaction limits if any.

Now that we've covered what coupons are, how to identify them, and some restrictions. Discussing how and where to find coupons is just as important as knowing coupon policies. Following the policies fully allow for trust and loyalty between shopper and store. The saying, it's not what you know but who you know, rolls right into couponing. Finding a great source willing to trade, sale or donate their unused coupons and newspapers is not as farfetched as you may be assuming. I have had the same locations donating their unused papers (coupon inserts) to me for the last three years. In 2013 I drove delivery for a local newspaper company part-time just to receive extras for free as an employee (I mean business about getting my coupons). Local businesses, stores, friends, family members and coworkers are all great starting points. If you live near a shopping strip of any sort their recycling bins are gold mines. Not wanting to leave the couch to get coupons?

Internet printable coupons are just what you need. The printing "restrictions" are very easy to manipulate to give endless quantities. I will only share this information in this writing. I did not and will not say this in class: In order to get an endless amount of coupons simply manipulate your computers printing options to always ask before printing. This simple task will pop-up your printing window each time your computer tries to send something to any printer on the same network. When that happens simply change the amount of copies you want printed. Magic! As I said, there should be no issue with any of you finding coupons or printing them.

Some people don't like to use internet printable coupons, I am not one of those people. I started with internet printable and they have always worked for me. People I've talked to state they don't like the hassle from store employees. This goes back to the topic of fraudulent coupons. Due to some people making fraudulent coupons, stores have started to scrutinize them more. I advise if you don't have a fraudulent coupon than it shouldn't be a hassle. They have a job to do, let them. If you have planned your trip correctly and followed store policy then there should not be an issue that can't be immediately resolved. I am adamant about being very polite to your cashiers and store managers. Especially if you want to take hundreds of dollar worth of groceries out the store for close to free. There is never any reason to be nasty with employees for questioning your actions. If they ask, answer without attitude or temper. I spent a lot of time preparing this course for many to benefit from. Please remember you are not the only couponer in your city and please don't give us a bad reputation for something that can be handled without argument. Those who don't like using internet

printables usually make habit of using clipping services. As much as I enjoy the concept of always having every coupon at your access at all times. I don't agree with paying for something that is initially free (coupon inserts are INCLUDED in the price of a newspaper). The newspaper company receives profit for their service not the manufacturer disturbing the insert, this is simply their means of mass disturbing. I want to make clear, I do not buy coupons. However, I don't judge those who do. I have researched it and each time found the coupon I was looking for and printed it myself. Free of charge. At certain times of the month I will stock up on ink because I know I will be doing a lot of printing. If you chose clipping services are more convenient for you then please research delivery timeframes and expiration dates before purchase. See resources page for list of clipping services.

Have you ever wondered why certain items never seem to go on sale or have a coupon offer? Yes, me too, I still wonder that at times. That's one question I didn't attempt to answer. The solution is simple; request a coupon, gift card or sample. It works every time! I first start by registering (phone call or email) a compliment of their products and ASK for a coupon. Simply, ask. Example: Hi, my name is Tonya I recently purchased your (name of product) and I wanted to just say it is the best thing I've used for (product purpose). I wish I had found this product years ago for (name special occasion associated with product or upcoming holiday). Do you have a coupon, gift card or sample you can send me? I would love to share it with my family at a (restate original occasion) scheduled for next weekend. They normally say yes, send you a coupon and that's the end of it. Some companies have a mailing list that receive coupons on a regular basis for a certain length of time. If you notice you haven't gotten your coupons as scheduled, call and make the request again.

Let's assume the call/email didn't go as well. Think to yourself; what is the first thing asked when calling a customer service company? I hope that was enough seconds to guess, but the answer is YOUR information. By the time you've offered such a great review for a company not to offer a reward of gratitude is just rude. Make sure they know that in a very stern yet disappointed manner. Example: Oh, you don't offer ANY of those things? Wow, well how does your company reward your customers' loyalty? Maybe they still claim not to offer coupons. Here's a great rebuttal I use before ending the call: Well I do appreciate you taking my call today. I will go ahead and use the (name top competitor of brand) brand for our (previously stated occasion). Hurry and end the call, if you are asked the golden question about taking a survey at the end of the call: SAY YES! In the survey answer honestly about the person's performance but when it gets to the question of recommending to others, SAY NO! This will trigger a customer retention alert and just about every business has an automated program that will start to send discount offers and, you guess it, coupons. From now on, always say you wouldn't recommend a service and you will soon be showered with gifts and goodies. I know it sounds misleading but the purpose of the course and the reason you attended was to learn about couponing. This is how you can get high dollar coupons that are usually sent directly to you and you only.

This brings us to how we all found each other: social media. As you all are well aware social media is taking the lead in communication and delivery. From the way we communicate to when we chose to communicate is satisfied instantly through social media sites. Television

I did this once to Samsung right before Christmas about three years ago. I ended up with a free 32 inch TV. Did you know you can get a free laptop? Making companies compete for your business is key to this type of reward. If you were to take a broken Microsoft laptop into Apple do you think they would offer a discount for your business? Not only is the answer yes, but if you were to "create" a scenario of being a "returning customer" you could walk away with a free MAC product no purchase necessary.

shows relay on social media as well as non-profit organizations seeking donations. Social media has, in some aspects, taken over what we knew of conversing with one another. This is also a great way to get exclusive coupons. By clicking a like button, retweet, or snap while on location your user profile is tracked from that moment. Notifications and alerts will offer limited and exclusive coupons usually offered on a very numbered inventory. Social media coupons are mainly first come first serve and limited to the amount of prints you can receive. However, remember my tip from previous page about overcoming that issue. Having covered the basics of coupon hunting please take the time to join as many shopper reward and internet cash back programs as possible. This is where you want to start for extreme couponing purposes. If you goal is to simply save money than join just a few you frequent. The information and directions are still the same. Once you have joined those programs go the products and manufacturer social media and web pages. Sign up for their mailing lists then proceed to make your registered compliments as mentioned. Once you've completed this you will see your coupon inventory increase within days. The compliment technique can be used for several products; including clothing, services, car repairs, and even restaurant eatery. Be sure to use this technique to gain rare and exclusive coupons and discounts. If not offered a coupon the first attempt, wait 10 business days and register a complaint.

When registering a complaint make sure to not over exaggerate the issue. Stating: I called on (date of compliment) offering praise of your product and company. At the time I requested a coupon to use for an upcoming (name of original event). I was told that couldn't be provided. At the (name of original event) my family and friends continuously asked me about your product because I had signed up to bring it for everyone to (purpose of product). This caused a lot of embarrassment and repeated questioning from others. I really wish you had offered a coupon. End the communication with a simple salutation. Of course, a statement like this is best recognized by the company when in written form. Make sure to mail or email this type of communication.

Tips: Join reward and cash back programs immediately. Locate your coupons through all techniques given. Create your own scenarios to gain access to rare and exclusive coupons. Use the same template email when registering compliments and complaints. Utilize company social media and web pages.

Pricing and Store Advertisements
With coupons in hand, freshly printed and/or clipped. Reward and cash back programs joined; you are now ready for the store ads. This is where couponing either gets fun or frustrating. The "two F's I give" when couponing is what I like to call them. You will come to points in time where you are fed up of trying to break the mathematical code to beat the register. There are times that it will be so easy to do that you'll feel like you're stealing. I want to be up front that couponing takes both time and effort. Extreme couponing takes: time, effort, planning, preparing, sweat, tears, and even hair (from the pulling). ← This is where you laugh out loud. Jokes aside, couponing is fun and rewarding. It benefits many and keeps stores gaining revenue. Even when it seems a store manager or cashier is getting frustrated with you, rest assure that they are still making a profit. Coupons or cash, they are both equally forms of payment.
When reviewing a stores ad be sure to also have their website up for price verification. I regularly view the ad and the website at the same time. This is to see additional purchasing options and product sizes. For example: Colgate twin packs are on sale for $6.99. Whereas the singles are regular price at $2.99. With a $1.00 off coupon the single product package is the better buy. Knowing what you learned about price competition, if $2.99 is regular price then you should actually save that $1.00 off coupon until that item is on sale. Also starting to learn your product suggested retail prices you find that price will probably be around $1.99 when on sale. Making better use of your $1.00 off coupon. You want to utilize the coupon but capitalize on the sale.

Once you have verified that you have the lowest possible offered price you can began to search for coupons for those items. It is easier to identify what coupons are readily available for a sale item than identifying what coupons have corresponding sales. There is always more coupons out than sale items advertised. Again, remember coupons aren't meant to benefit you they are meant to retain your business. You want to start by completely reading the ENTIRE coupon. Leave nothing out, this is for your own benefit and knowledge. If asked about any of your coupons at register be ready to answer quickly and without having to review them again. Shop with confidence that you have selected the right coupon and therefore items also. Again reread the store's coupon policy. You do not want any surprise changes that will cost you money. I normally start by going through the store ad front cover to back while writing down the known coupons available for each sale item. Once I have completed that task I do the math finding the highest coupon combination causing the lowest price. I do this for each store every week prior to planning a trip. This keeps the prices fresh in your mind and readily available for future use.

When pricing products make sure to research the cost. Just because Walgreen's is running a sale doesn't mean that Walmart everyday low price is lowest between the two. Just because it says sale does not mean that it is the lowest price. Knowing your stores is one of the major requirements to extreme couponing. From the aisle of which a product is located to the normally listed sales price is beneficial for you. What benefits you is what saves you money at the check-out lane. Make sure to make your own sales on items when needed by using combinations of savings available. I recommend at times to ask customer service desk for a "product/inventory list." They don't make habit of handing these out so don't be surprised if you are denied. Most may direct you to their website; which is why I've said stalk their websites!

Using a coupon on a clearance or already discounted item? Is it possible? Yes, and yes! Using a coupon on these items usually causes the system to "overload." When a company places something on clearance that is usually at a store level decision. A lot of times there is nothing wrong with the product, they just want the shelf space for a different product. When that happens; we have fun! Because the store has changed the price they also have manipulated the original coding of the barcode. This manipulation makes the system fail to recognize if you indeed purchased the correct quantity as stated on the coupon. This causes the full coupon to apply to the total purchase not just the total item cost. Example: Toothpaste is on clearance for 50¢ and you have a $1.00 off 1 coupon. You will actually be able to get two item with one coupon face value. The register is "supposed" to identify the new price at 50¢. However when the store manipulated the bar code they removed the quantity code so no more of the product is ordered for their store. Being that the new quantity code is entered as 0 when coupon is scanned it can't read the quantity you purchased only the manufacturer's code. This results in what a couponer calls overage. Because the overage was caused at the transaction level then the discount will actually apply to any product added from that same manufacturer product line. This is how you can also get discounts applied to non-coupon bearing items. How do you know when this will happen? The answer is: trial and error. Knowing your store is key!

Planning a Shopping Trip and Grocery List
Always start your planning with a clear view of what is on sale, where it is on sale, any offered rewards or cash back, all coupon combinations available, and the cost of the item. This organization will help you to stay on track without getting distracted by shining objects (other sales). Another great idea is having a list of what you know your family/household already needs. Let's not start out obsessively buying just yet. Give yourself some time to learn the best techniques for you, before you start to bulk buy. This advice is simply to caution of disappointed trips. Staying on track with what is on sale and by researching your buying scenarios prior to shopping will actually save you more money. It does take more time but time is money. You can't waste time planning a trip, it's not possible. Detailed planning can only result in the best scenario discoveries.
When you have found at least two different manufacturer coupon options per product, search for in-store coupons for the same item. Also look for digital coupons, shopper reward perks, and cash back options. The process is known as stacking coupons. The outcome is a deeper savings per item. Per item savings is what leads to overages. Stacking coupon gives you final cost per item prior to adding to shopping list. Once you have figured the math and find your stock-up price, then stock-up!

Organizing your coupons at checkout from highest amount to lowest will also provide added savings. When you remove a high dollar coupon first it triggers on the lowest cost first. Making that item free first. Very important: after all products and coupons have been scanned, politely ask the cashier to give subtotal. This helps verify that you are on track then enter you shopper ID number. If there is an error at this point it can be considered at store level and easily corrected at the service desk. If you find a store discount did not apply than you can go to the service desk and show the receipt of price paid and they will gladly correct the price mismatch. This also helps so there is no rejecting of your physical coupon due to a digital coupon. This is to not "confuse" the system or cashier. This technique will actually show full savings received not just sale pricing.

When making large quantity purchases sometimes it is best to alert your store ahead of time. This will one, make sure the items are available. And two, leave some items for in-store inventory. A lot of times I will do this when bulk buying pasta or toothpaste. It does not cost to order and it does not have to be paid for up front. They may question why you need that many of one thing, "create" a story. Best policy is to NOT mention that you will be couponing for the items. Once you've done this successfully a few times the store won't even question you when requested. Which leads more to my number one rule: DO NOT CLEAR THE SHELF! BE CONSIDERATE OF OTHERS. Sorry for the caps, but it is a pet peeve to see a couponer clearing a shelf only to go to a car filled with the same item. Grinds my gears.

A lot of people will coupon by splitting their transactions. Although in some cases it is needed, depending on the store and coupon this actually might be the worst thing to do. If you have coupons that will cause a $5 overage on a toothpaste purchases then add other products and coupons that also have an overage to continue the purchase. That first overage of $5 is now causing a ripple effect throughout your shopping list. This is extreme couponing. You only want to split up transactions to avoid coupon limits per purchase. I cannot stress enough, knowing your store and reading your coupons will eliminate any room for error. When you identify an overage it is best to start combining items per coupon or mix/match buying. If you already have an overage and you next product to purchase is a $2 off 2 item, go ahead and see if getting 3 per coupon will push those items making them free. Or even better, causing another overage, when that happens use another item and set of coupons to do the exact same thing. Repeat until total is $0. *See coupon breakdown in tips section.

When your math is complete and coupons chosen I find it best practice to write a list. I personally have a very detailed list. As you know I learned how to figure prices and discounts when there wasn't a smart phone app readily available. Although this works for myself and others you may not need to be as detailed. In your list be sure to include the product, the sale price, and the number of coupons needed to be

scanned for per transaction. Following those tips will at least keep you organized while in store. You've heard of the Dryer Fairy; well there's a Coupon Fairy also. She flies out the sky and snatches your coupons while your back is turned unless you have them secure and safe. Be afraid of her, very afraid.

Once you have a list, check it, check it again, and then execute! When in store go directly to the products you have on your list. Be sure of sizing and packaging requirements. Especially in the beginning. You will eventually learn your own way and tricks to getting around some of those seemingly unnecessary requirements and restrictions. Trust me you will develop your own skill set. No one person coupons alike. I went with a fellow couponer and she completely stressed me out within five minutes because of her disorganization. I'm sure to her there was a method; I didn't see it. Just know that you will be told several times what you "could of, should of, and need to do." Let the helpful, help and the rest ignore. Follow what you know and are comfortable with. The first time is the most nerve wrecking because you may start to second guess yourself. Don't worry, this is normal. However, do not divert from the plan.

Organize your cart in a fashion that the items are neat and able to visually counted and scanned. This is especially true for large items. I also tend not to bag items when I have purchased in bulk. It just adds to the time spent in store. Make your purchase and leave, no need to linger. I say this so you don't wander the store looking for more deals. Once that first trip is a success you will immediately want to turn around and do it again. Be cautious is all I can offer to that temptation. I fight it at times too. Remember why you first started couponing is my advice. Sticking to your list while in store ensures you don't manipulate your own purchase plan. As you will find, getting a good scenario is golden and you don't want to mess it up once you've gotten it. Adding products to an already set scenario can throw the entire transaction off. I recommend that if you find an item that is unbeatable, get it. Just do so on a separate purchase. Therefore if it doesn't come out properly, it's easier to return just that purchase than do so within you planned list.

At the Checkout
The number one rule of the checkout is actually before you get to the checkout. Make a wise decision on the cashier on choice. I never recommend older woman or veteran employees. I love the new young guy out of college for the summer. He's my man! Chatty Kathy's (sorry Kathy) are also great, they usually are in awe the whole time. My all-time favorite are the unimpressed. The one's who really look like they are chained to their registers underneath the counter: golden. They don't care about anything, if they can force a coupon, they will. What is most important about your cashier is either one of familiarity or one that is young. New employees are iffy at times. You have some that value their jobs and will scrutinize your transaction throughout. Others, the unimpressed, will give you the items and take them to your car. They just want to end their shift.
Personally I use the self-scan registers. This allows me to see the transaction first hand, no surprises. In this case the machine asks you to either scan your coupon or give it to the attendant. If an attendant is needed they will come and scan the item for you. I have yet to see any check or verify items prior to attempting to scan. Cashiers are trained that if a coupon scans it is acceptable, no questions asked. Not because some don't know what I am sharing but because that is what the store trains. Remember I the cashier and later in life, bank teller. Cashiers are told to verify the items by scanning the coupon. Rarely do cashiers verify the item prior to scanning because they don't require them until afterward.

As planned give your cashier the needed coupons you've already planned for *and a couple more but on the very bottom of the pile. Just to see what happens of course. Sometimes the system keeps scanning, this again is in your favor. Remember coupons are a form of payment and as with dollars; sometimes they will take as many as you give. If it doesn't scan it will be returned to you. Just apologize as an honest mistake. Thank them for returning it to you and continue your transaction. If the total does not equate to what you predicted then you only have seconds to decide what to do. Do quick math, or add another product. I like to choose candy bars right there for the lane. Sometimes all that's needed is another item to be scanned. These items are referred to as filler items.

Filler items are always best under $1.00 and if they have a coupon better. However, the purpose of a filler item is to give that extra item count on your transaction to use another coupon. Remembering coupons are scanned on a per item basis. Just add a couple of filler items and the amount should correct. If it does not, there is always the option to void and start over. Or pay and immediately go to service desk. Most times they are directed to offer refund if the amount is under a certain total. $5.00 is most thresholds, make sure the error is less than that before choosing to pay for transaction.

I want to again stress the importance of preparing in some way. You don't want to be at the cashier expecting one total and seeing another. The most common reason for this is because of reward points. When figuring prices at home do not include reward points in the final cost predictions. Only figure in reward points once they have been awarded. This is the same with Catalina coupons. Catalina coupons can be used from store to store. It does not matter if it says Walgreens, Meijer will accept it. It is a manufacturer coupon printed out at the register as a reward for the customer. Make sure you are getting your Catalina.

This brings me to travel and buddy shopping! Yes, travel. Don't let the city limits hold you back. A lot of times stores in smaller towns love to see the madness of coupons happen. They may limit your quantities but it's usually always worth the drive. They usually still have older systems with fewer restrictions. When you can find those stores be respectful to the small communities near them and do not clear their shelves. However, many of these stores still multiply coupons this is an added bonus when you still receive credit for you cash back programs and apps. Be sure to have joined these programs as an added opportunity to save money. They will send cash back or a variety of choices in gift cards. Once you receive your first pay-out, shopping goals become easier to accomplish. Remember these programs are to "multiply" your own coupons. More times than none, the cash back rewards are offered on already on sale products.

Storing Your Products

Storing your products is so much fun and at times time consuming. I started out just by emptying a hall closet and stocking it. After about a two months it was filled. Then I went to the garage, then the basement. Before I knew it products were even under the beds. My best direction for this is to at least organize your products. Have an area for each group of items i.e. Household, hygiene care, food, and laundry. This is important: if you have a pet; hide your pet products. You don't want to come home to torn open dog food bags. It's not fun and even 3 pound Pomeranians figure it out. If you have small children; please keep items out of their reach. Please.

I have evolved to shelving. It is more convenient and takes up less space. I even couponed my shelfs. Yes I did. When you learn how to cause an overage you will enjoy the perks of getting free items also. Make use of you overages and rewards. I use overages, rewards, and cash back on items and services that do not ever offer coupons. I love the clearance section and that is where I find a lot of my organizational items that are needed when couponing.

Covering organization is a personal task that must be accomplished. A disorganized couponer is obvious. You can spot them a mile away. They are the ones still looking for coupons while items are being scanned. These couponers were my worst remember as a teenager. I had to do all the work for them, which was not my job description. So be courteous and be organized, especially at the checkout. Organizing coupons are just as important so organizing you products. You don't want to print or order coupons you already own. Likewise, you don't want to waste money or time when you have the coupon at along. Make sure to use what works best for you. I used binders for years, only because I am a little OCD. No other real reason besides that. I rarely took my binders with me, they were for simple home use. More like a filing system to me. Which led me to file folders. I enjoy those because I don't have to cut the coupon prior to filing. Again, use what works best for you.

At this point it is best to also point out you purpose of couponing. Being you are reading this manual I can make the assumption it was for personal reasons. Only you know the true reason or details. We won't ignore the fact that some people get into couponing for profit or business ventures. I never wanted that to be a part of what I did. However, here we are. It is a marketable business, yes, but it was never my intention. I have done this for so long that people ask me how all the time. I realized I was giving away my skill set for free. I realized more importantly I was giving away my time for free. I had to accept that I was living two standards: one of saving money or the other of wasting my time. Very contradictory. I put all this together with hopes that you all would not just learn from me but become your own shopper. A better shopper. That is now my goal in couponing. Know yours.

If you joined couponing to gain profit from the start by selling your products I have some advice I'd like to offer. I again do not sell but I do not judge those who do. They too have put in time and effort toward beginning a savings to you without tax or middleman. They too have invested to begin you products. I do respect what they do and how. I only offer that you not bundle items. I have never understood the concept of "these are the items you get, pay me." The joy of shopping and hence getting a great deals is that YOU get a choice. I have sensitive skin, you cannot tell me what laundry detergent to buy. If you bundle: make a bundle price guide not an actual bundle. Example: $25 includes a detergent, dryer sheets, dish liquid, 4 body washes. And so on, but please stop selling the here's a picture bundles; gains my gears. Your purpose as a business owner is to make your customer happy. Happy is not you choosing their items and wanting payment. Give you customers' choices and they will choose.

If you decide to do pop up or even open a store, please look into the laws of selling items that have been purchased with coupons in a retail environment. I have never researched this topic and never will. As stated, you will find you own way. Utilize what you learn to the fullest and cover yourself from liabilities. Once you have learned your own personal touch to couponing you will absolutely start to think more strongly about investing and capitalizing on what you know. Again it is a marketable entity.

With profits and selling talk out the way I want to discuss my way of getting rid of products I will never use. You will make habit of getting these items because they usually are the items that give you overages. For my family those items are few. I am the eldest sibling of 17; we aren't wasteful by any means. Almost everything on the market; at least one of my family members could use. I give a lot to them. My store is their store. Any other items that I can't seem to use or give away I donate to charity. I don't have a favorite; I donate to all. At Thanksgiving my family and I go downtown and give out hygiene bags. At Christmas; food bags.

What to do with coupons you don't need? Share, sale, or trade. Just as you are searching someone else is also. Use coupon groups and websites to locate what you want and give up what you don't. This will keep you coupon stock full and at the ready. If you have expiring coupons please use in a recycling manner. I wouldn't recommend trying to use them but do understand the store is still paid for them 90 days after expiration. Now get to planning, this is it. The end!

In conclusion
Please utilize this manual as much as needed. Also join our Facebook group for help and tips from others. We are a new group but already passed 100 members in just the first day. I have many couponing friends in the group also, take their advice, it's worth it. See the resources, tips, breakdowns, and steps pages at the end of this manual. I want to thank you all from the bottom of my heart. This journey has been both rewarding and overwhelming. I mean that in a good way. I have been very overwhelmed with support and encouragement. I cannot thank you all enough. I feel like I have started a new journey in my life with couponing and I welcome it fully. I don't always like change or putting myself in a vulnerable position. However, you all in one way or another eased those concerns. Again, I thank you. Please go shop now: I'm tired of typing and I want to shop. All this talk of shopping; I want to shop. See you all in group.
Donten Vyme
Coupon Envy

10 STEPS TO COUPON

1. **Gather weekly store ads** for all your local grocery stores. Meijer, Kroger, Walmart, Dollar General, Family Dollar, Walgreens, CVS, and Target. By item and page figure out what has a readily available coupon. Write that coupon value on the ad for quick reference later in planning.

2. Be sure to **identify the regional low prices** for sale items. Those that are not at lowest price offering save for later or use as filler items. The purpose here is to find the rock bottom prices of the week that have corresponding coupons, rewards and cash back scenarios. Again for quick reference throughout the week.

3. **Find/Locate/Purchase needed coupons** for the entire week all at once. Best time to order coupons is on Sunday nights/Monday mornings for faster shipment. Make use of whatever routine works best for you. Internet printables are accepted in Fort Wayne region. Check your regions for sure.

4. **Make shopping breakdown**. Work your math until it is at the absolute lowest price. A way to verify your math is add another item and coupon. See if the price decreases or increases. If it increases you have found your best scenario. Remember not everyone will have the same coupons, therefore cannot make the same purchases. Stick to it! If other purchases need to be made due to surprise clearance or sale; make a separate transaction. Set a savings goal as well as a couponing budget. Couponing can be so cheap that you don't realize you've spent hundreds of dollars by weeks end. Make a daily couponing budget and stick with it! As you progress make it a weekly budget. Mine is set at $50 a week and has been for years. I do not shop every week.

5. **Checklist prior to leaving home**. Make sure to have all coupons ready and organized. Have shopping list prepared and also available throughout trip. This is to make sure you grab the correct number of each needed item for your transaction. This is the perfect time to double check any digital coupons and reward offerings. Make sure they are clipped/uploaded PRIOR to shopping. You don't want to miss out on those discounts that is what the make or break your transaction. Do not depend on their website once in store. Several times I have been unable to get service inside certain stores. Cashiers also won't take a screenshot of coupon, it must be uploaded.

6. **Go directly to items once in store**. Organize your cart so items are easily counted and visible. Get more than one cart if necessary. You want your items to ring up most expensive items first. As well as have you coupons organized by highest face value first. Remember this tip. Once items are scanned asked for subtotal, then hand over coupons and asked to be scanned in order please. Remember the please. After coupons are scanned enter in your shopper rewards ID. Watch the prices fall. A beautiful sight. Choose your cashier wisely.

7. **Organize and store haul**. Remember to keep items out of reach of small children and pets. We don't want any horrible accidents. Manager your receipts for uploading to cash back programs. Value your receipts, they are money at this point in the game also. Pick up dropped receipts, I love those. Count and inventory your products. No need to overload, this will eventually add to wasted and expired products.

8. Now that receipts are organized. **Find cash back programs** for those items. Submit all reward request and wait. Choose the best pay out option for you. I love cash. Although gift cards are fun and great for the holidays.

9. **Verify your shopper rewards program** with local stores. Make sure items used credited correctly. This is the time when they may be a chance to add that same reward back, if so do it immediately. Sometimes it does take the system awhile to read purchases. Be patience.

10. **DO IT ALL OVER AGAIN!**

- Join shopper reward and cash back programs for all your favorite stores immediately. Kroger, Dollar General, Meijer, CVS, Family Dollar, Target, Walgreens *Walmart does not have a digital program.
- Find coupons! As many as possible as quick as possible. Request them! Clipping services are fast but printing services are faster. Verify with your store's website what coupons are accepted prior to trip.
- Which bring us to: Know you store's coupon policy. Make sure you check them on a regular basis. At least once a month, just to be careful.
- Organize your coupons and products in an inventory style for space saving. Locate a place in your home to store products as their package design requires. Caution on storing things in places like outdoor sheds and unsecure out buildings of the likeliness. You don't want thieves around.
- Join social media and internet groups for tips, directions, and scenarios. A lot of these sites offer pretty good breakdowns. But remember there are some things you won't learn on the web. Some things are learned by simply trying it out. Always recheck their math and verify you can actually get your hands on the coupon prior to sale end date.
- Set aside a designated time to coupon. Let it be daily or weekly; make sure to set aside a certain amount of time as to remain productive in other areas of life outside of couponing. For those that make a living from couponing by all means, work.
- Become a master at fighting overage scenarios. These are you money makers. The reason you put in some much work with price scenarios is for this benefit. The reason you coupon is because of overages; so learn them. Practice makes perfect.
- Don't get frustrated and give up. Ask for help. If you can see the numbers but can't figure them out, ask. There's a community for a reason. Reach out to them. Buddy group shopping is absolutely awesome. However make sure to find someone who has the same style as you. The last thing you want is each other picking apart the others method and purchase.
- BE KIND! Be welcoming and up beat when couponing. If trouble happens let it happen knowing there's another day, another store. Don't argue with store personnel it only makes us all look bad. If they are rude, remember you are a normal customer and deserve to be treated as such. Report the incident the proper way and follow chain of command. Don't be aggressive but don't be a push over easy. If you know you are correct and can prove it without argument or tension; do so.
- Know your store coupon policy, if that's repeated: it's because it's that important.

RESOURCES: Where's my coupon?

PRINTABLES	CLIPPING SERVICES
Coupons.com KrazyCouponLady.com Target.com Walmart.com PG.com Meijer.com Grocerycouponnetwork.com Grocerycouponcart.com Savewith.coupons.com Smartsource.com Smartsource.ca PG.ca Couponsforprint.com Couponmom.com Visit any manufacturer website and social media pages. Simply Google (item) coupons and you'll find plenty if available.	Coupon Clippers Coupon Flea Market Klip2Save Stock Piling Moms The Coupon Carry Out Jacks Cards and Coupons West Coast Coupon Clipping We Clip You Save Daily Dimes Bargain Coupon Clipper We Coupon Clipz Google again and find you right price for your personal budget.
HOW TO PRINT Use your overages to stock up on printing Use black and white ink, no need for color Recycle paper, use every space Do not print double sided Manipulate printer options to queue pop-up permission screen Get a wireless printer, these are best for networking purposes Use your local library and save money and time Print as many as needed the first time, the coupon may disappear	**REQUESTING COUPONS** Visit company and manufacturer websites and request coupons and samples All samples are accompanied by a coupon for purchase Follow the compliment/complaint method Take all surveys when offered Join mailing list MAKE SURE TO MAKE SEVERAL EMAIL AND REWARD PROGRAMS ID'S.

PRICE BREAKDOWN EXAMPES

⌐ **Bought 3 Crest Pro-Health Toothpaste, 3.3 oz. $2.99, sale price through 9/23**
* *Buy 3, Receive $3.00 Register Reward through 9/23*
Used two $2.00/1 – Crest Toothpaste 3 oz. or more from SS 9/17
* And used one $2.00/1 – Crest Toothpaste, 3 oz. or larger, manufacturer eCoupon (walgreens.com)
And submitted three $0.25/1 – Crest Pro-Health, 3 oz. or larger, via rebate app (ibotta.com)
Paid $2.97, Received $3.00 Register Reward and Submitted for $0.75 in Ibotta Credits
Final Price: $0.78 Moneymaker

⌐ **Bought 2 Children's Advil, 24 ct () $2.79, clearance price**
Used two $1.00/1 – Advil product (advil.com)
Or $1.00/1 – Advil Infants' or Children's, Robitussin Children's or Dimetapp from RP 8/20
* And used one $3.00/2 – Robitussin, 4 oz., Dimetapp, 4 oz., Children's Advil, 24 ct or Liquid, 4 oz. or Infants' Drops, 0.5 oz. from Walgreens September Savings Book (expr 9/30)
Final Price: $0.58

⌐ **Bought 2 Colgate Total Mouthwash, 8.4 oz. $3.99, regular price**
* *Buy One Get One 50% Off through 9/23*
Buy 2, Receive 3,000 Balance Rewards Points through 9/23
Used two $1.00/1 – Colgate Mouthwash or Mouth Rinse 200 mL or larger from SS 9/10
Paid $3.99, Received 3,000 Balance Rewards Points ($3.00)
Final Price: $0.99

⌐ **Bought 2 Garnier Fructis Shampoo, Conditioner or Styler, 12 or 12.5 or 2-8.5 oz. $3.50 each, when you buy 2, sale price through 9/23**
Used one $4.00/2 – Garnier Fructis Shampoo, Conditioner or Treatment from RP 8/27
* And used one $2.00/2 – Garnier Fructis Hair Care Shampoo or Conditioner, 10.2-12.5 oz. or Stylers and Treatments, 2-8.5 oz. form Walgreens September Savings Book (expr 9/30)
Final Price: $1.00

⌐ **Bought 2 Reese's Peanut Butter Pumpkin, 1.2 oz. $0.75 each, when you buy 2, sale price through 9/23**

- **Or Kit Kat Trick or Treat Bars, 1.55 oz. $0.75 each, when you buy 2, sale price through 9/23**
  Or Cadbury Screme Egg, 1.2 oz. $0.75 each, when you buy 2, sale price through 9/23
- Used one $0.50/2 – Hershey's or Cadbury Halloween Singles Candy, 1.2-3.5 oz. from Walgreens September Savings Book (expr 9/30)

Final Price: $1.00

Bought 2 Pond's Facial Towelettes, 15 ct $3.79, regular price
- *Buy One Get One Free through 9/23*
  Buy 2, Receive 2,000 Balance Rewards Points through 9/23

Paid $3.79, Received 2,000 Balance Rewards Points ($2.00)

Final Price: $1.79

TOTAL PRICE $4.58 RETAIL $46.08 UNTIL 9/23/2017

Bought 1 Crest Pro-Health Toothpaste, 4.6 oz. $2.99, regular price

Used one $2.00/1 – Crest Toothpaste 3 oz. or more from SS 9/17
And submitted one $1.00/1 – Crest Toothpaste, 3 oz. or larger, via rebate app(ibotta.com)
Paid $0.99, Submitted for $1.00 Ibotta Credit

Final Price: $0.01 Moneymaker

Bought 1 Crest Complete Toothpaste, 5.8-6.2 oz. $2.99, regular price

Used one $2.00/1 – Crest Toothpaste 3 oz. or more from SS 9/17
And submitted one $1.00/1 – Crest Toothpaste, 3 oz. or larger, via rebate app(ibotta.com)
Paid $0.99, Submitted for $1.00 Ibotta Credit

Final Price: $0.01 Moneymaker

Bought 1 Crest 3D White Toothpaste, 3.5 oz. $2.99, regular price

Used one $2.00/1 – Crest Toothpaste 3 oz. or more from SS 9/17
And submitted one $1.00/1 – Crest Toothpaste, 3 oz. or larger, via rebate app(ibotta.com)
Paid $0.99, Submitted for $1.00 Ibotta Credit

Final Price: $0.01 Moneymaker

Bought 1 Bic Simply Soleil Razors, 3 ct $3.27, regular price

Used one $3.00/1 – BIC Soleil Disposable Razor Pack (excludes trial and travel sizes)(coupons.com)

Final Price: $0.27

Bought 1 Lysol 10X Power Toilet Bowl Cleaner, 1 ct $1.97, regular price
Bought 1 Lysol Automatic Toilet Bowl Cleaner, 1 ct $1.77, regular price

Used one $1.00/2 – Lysol Toilet Bowl Cleaners from SS 8/27

And submitted one $0.75/1 – Lysol Automatic Toilet Bowl Cleaner, 1.37 oz., via rebate app (checkout51.com)
And submitted one $0.75/1 – Lysol Automatic Toilet Bowl Cleaner, 1.37 oz., via rebate app (checkout51.com)
And received bonus $0.75/1 – Lysol Bonus, when you buy both, via rebate app (checkout51.com)
Paid $2.74, Submitted for $1.50 in Checkout 51 Credits and $0.75 Checkout 51 Bonus
Final Price: $0.49
TOTAL COST 73¢ WALMART DEAL ENDING 9/23/17

Coupon "Lingo"

Sunday inserts:

P&G = Procter & Gamble Sunday insert

RP = RedPlum Sunday insert

SS = SmartSource Sunday insert

Lingo:

MFG- Manufacture coupon

blinkie- those red flashing things in the stores that give out coupons

BOGO-Buy one Get one FREE

B2G1- buy two get one FREE

YAG-Yellow Advantage Flyer

GAF- Green Advantage Flyer

Q's- Coupons

$1/2 - one dollar off of two

$1/1- one dollar off of one!!!

exp- expires

Ea- Each

ECB: Extra Care Bucks (CVS)

GC- Gift card

IVC- Instant Value Coupon

OOP- Out of pocket

OOS- Out of Stock

MIR- Mail in Rebate

Peelie- The stickers on products that are coupons

WYB- When you buy

Tearpad: Pad of coupons attached to a display, shelf, or refrigerator door.

UPC: Universal product code, bar code

www.ingramcontent.com/pod-product-compliance
Lightning Source LLC
Chambersburg PA
CBHW040246240726
48664CB00001B/284